1

Table of Contents

The Vanguard Faction

A Novel By Al R Suarez

Intro

This book is dedicated to the great Uruguayan revolutionary poet and writer, Eduardo Galeano, who died earlier this year (2015). It has turned into a custom since my first book to dedicate my book to ones that have passed. My third book expands on The Unfinished Revolution into the importance of the vanguard to the movement. The vanguard is the youth, the center, the source, of the generational struggle, it is the very essence or core of the revolutionary phase. The rebellion phase, as we see in the streets of Baltimore today, is a pre revolutionary scenario. Revolutions are systems or process, or counter processes, to counter balance the injustice or oppression based on the conditions of the society it is trying to replace with a new society.

Not to be confused with an elite force, which has at times been distorted based on the initial intention of vanguard, the vanguard are ones who coordinate or lead and facilitate the implementation of revolutionary programs. Usually a small foco, these groups work together and focus on the working or affinity groups and fulfilling their various tasks. During occupy, a vanguard was initially being formed, but was eventually sabotaged, principally because of infiltration and a lack of organization as discussed in my two previous books.

Vanguardists in every nation strive to accomplish aims, for a society void of borders, the essence of internationalism. If we see the struggle in Tahrir (Egypt) we see the vanguard were infiltrated by MB (Muslim Brotherhood) and agents of the military and Mubarak himself. Today Mubarak has been pardoned and we have a man who is in many ways more tyrannical than Mubarak who has taken over (Sisi). His treatment of the Palestinian question leaves no doubt he takes orders directly from Tel-Aviv and Washington. We must prevent in our revolution in the developed society of the US a Napoleon, Stalin or Sisi coming about. The cult of personality must be discouraged, and we must build a counter culture based on egalitarianism and social justice. For this the vanguard is needed, an important aspect of the revolutionary struggle, quite vital and crucial for the survival of the movement. As tactics cannot even be discussed or adapted without the role of the vanguard. It would be like having a vehicle, it may look good, but it cannot move without the gasoline, the energy or power used to propel or progress the movement is that which is brought by the spirit of the vanguard. This book is intended to be sold for a more economical price than the last two, with an emphasis on readership from the working class. In fact in forums it is encouraged to be given for free by those who genuinely are interested.

Chapter 1

The Manifesto & Commentaries

The following is a manifesto I wrote in 2014 with a comrade who is part of the leadership of the Revolutionary Liberation Party, a group I started in 2010 upon my return to the States from Europe.

"2020 Vision: 6 year Plan Manifesto

July 12, 2014 at 11:32pm

By Chris Jackson Rojas & Al R Suarez

We envision 6 years from now the revolutionary tasks that are needed to be implemented towards the new society, will be more attainable and applicable, invariably helping to better the conditions on the ground and exerting the maximum effort on local government for real, revolutionary change, and revolutionary transformative scenarios instead of reform which is fake change. The new era of progress is upon us, and the youth must unite and be the vanguard in the rebellion towards a revolution, starting with a revolution of consciousness. We must lead by example and discipline and ready ourselves for the revolutionary phase.

The student debt issue in particular, which is acquired in order for most of the youth to get a College degree here in the US, is an intentional policy as to distract the graduated students with the issue of paying back the State and getting work, instead of organizing for changing the system or status quo imposed upon us. To have a freethinking society it is necessary that questioning of authority is accepted and in fact encouraged in academia, when all too often the contrary, obedience, is what is taught and instilled in the youth. The 2020 vision is a vision of clarity which will help inspire the masses into action based on the consciousness which has shown that the injustice, classicism, racism, sexism, unemployment, discrimination, and Police State measures, will be combated with a counter force.

Counter culture, to combat selfishness and oneness with a collectivized society of sharing and selflessness, must come about when building the new society. We want to unite the third party people, the radicals, the revolutionaries, under the banner of social justice, equality, and Socialism, towards a democratic platform to bring real and permanent change that is needed for the very survival of humanity.

The whole idea of the 2020 vision is a reboot of government in the United States, and elsewhere. When it comes to the United States it is a reboot not by reform or by an oxymoron radical reform, as reboot by reform is impossible, that task would be asking the government to self-destruct, an action which won't happen.

We believe that we are anti-fascists acting in a matter like anti-fascists before us, removing the doctrine of evil, the idea that corporations and an authoritarian state should be merged. Fascist governments act as an expanding corporation via globalism, as in fascism the government is comprised of profiteers that have no regard for the very essence of humanity. The fascist government with imperialist-Machiavellian type strategy spreads their brand around the globe, fascism is an infectious disease, that getting stronger it gains severity, and can become a de facto Military Junta. This disease and all its systems must be cured, this cancer can be driven out with Socialism.

The workers are most in danger as fair pay for labor does not equal profit to the extent that the profiteers that are associates or the very politicians themselves in the criminal cartel, lust for profit. The workers are either enticed or divided as we have been for much of history. The enticement is the bait of a nearly fictional "American Dream", when in reality the majority of the wealth is acquired by an elite, is money that is inherited, because of the fictional dream, many of the workers do not turn on the power structures that repress them, and use the fruits of their labor, to gain even more profit causing the gaping crevice between worker, and CEO so wide, that it is nearly unfathomable.

The Second is division, the workers remain in a system owned by corporations divided via many ways. There is race, which those race relations appearing mended, the tension still exists, and in fact racism towards Middle Easterners, Hispanics, and Russians has gained strength. There is the false democrat-republican paradigm when in fact both parties are one, protecting the military-industrial complex. There is the generation divisions leaving a young and old worker very divided. There is division by petty issues portrayed in the media often to cause a rift, as fight over methods in-spite of having the same aims, continues, and the State takes advantage and tries to divide and conquer.

Any attempts at a revolution will be repressed, via covert infiltration, and in a succinct and clandestine matter, the revolution will be over by assassinations, financial targeting, and false flag operations if the government deems necessary. The workers must be willing to be dedicated in revolution, and the idea of a militia may seem excessively violent, however defense of the workers is important, violence should never be a first option, but quote on quote "peaceful opposition" can only work as long as your enemy remains peaceful, a militia needs to be organized, and a counter-intelligence force made, as covert infiltrators will be ubiquitous.

In the final analysis, by the year 2020 we hope to see the conditions made to better the way for a real revolution from the most developed country in the world, the US, which can spread towards a worldwide movement for a new era is upon us. Getting rid of the electoral college, participation in presidential debates, a more inclusive system of independents and third party people, are all ways to help us on our path. Bettering the public education system in high school, stopping the military recruiters and indoctrination. Bringing besides public health care, not Obamacare, public university programs, so as to prevent student debt, are all steps in the right direction. Other developed nations have already acquired these rights. We must demand and not ask, the time for reform is over."

As 2015 approached we saw with Dean Capone, who Chris and I met in Florida, backing out as running for president with the Socialist Party USA (who only has about 1000 members in total who pay dues and are barely on the ballot), and with Bernie Sanders who we wanted comrades about, emerging as a Democrat to run for president, that the left needs leadership now more than ever. A united front party to organize the masses is necessary as we see Syriza (Greece), Podemos (Spain) and parties in Latin America organize and win successfully.

KshamaSawant in Seattle turned from a radical Socialist to a Democrat much like Sanders, and the left is getting more and more disenchanted. The Greens on many issues have a liberal rather than radical view such as gun rights, so who is left of the independents or third parties of the left who is revolutionary? This is something the faction of factions, the vanguard, must take up and face head on.

Chapter 2

The Philadelphia Example

The following is an article I wrote that I hope will be published in The People's Tribune by the time this book comes out. Although I have differences with Stein I have much respect for the woman who was her running mate with the Green Party USA in 2012 Cheri Honkala, who lives in Philly and is mentioned in the article, following the article I will explain the example of Philly and how it is relevant to the revolutionary vanguard we are forming.

"The Revival in Philly: My Experience at the historic US Social Forum (26th-28th of June)

June 30, 2015 at 2:33pm

This article will be published in the People's Tribune, also to be translated to Spanish in El Tribuno del Pueblo.*

Meeting with celebrity activist rappers like Immortal Technique, and Rebel Diaz, may have been what you would expect to be the highlights of such a trip I took from Florida to Philadelphia to be at this summer's US Social Forum, however my encounters with them were brief, they were not in the march, and when you meet them, you see they are activists just like you. The encounters with them were great, but I met many extraordinary people from all over the world fighting in the same struggle for the same cause as me. I met comrades from Honduras, Peru, Montreal, Quebec, Paris, France, Ghana, Africa, from Kentucky, from Boston, from Florida, from all over, all who came to the US Social Forum to continue in their activism to bring radical revolutionary change, as I saw the revival of activism like in Occupy days come out in the great city of Philadelphia, in whose name is Greek in origin, the city of brotherly love, where the declaration of independence was written, the hometown of Benjamin Franklin, Mumia Abu Jamal, and Noam Chomsky.

Besides those prominent names the name of Cheri Honkala should be a household name for all activists. She lives in Philly and helped revive the Poor Peoples Economic Human Rights Campaign (PPEHRC) which was started by Dr. King. She also happened to have run for vice president of the US with the Green Party in 2012. Cheri led the march we had on Saturday,along with homeless and poor people, especially people of color, some were part of the Black Lives Matter movement, others were local people Cheri was helping. People from the ghetto, from Kensington, in the area near north Philly where Temple University is, who hosted us, were present. Cheri told us the case of the 14 year old boy dying of cancer, who the Emergency Assistance people in downtown Philly has still refused to house, as they and others have not housed a single family in 5 years, as they continue to hoard tax dollars and corruption continues. That is why from north Philly we marched to their office in downtown to protest the fact families are dying on the street or being sent to the church Cheri helps run in Kensington, instead of providing the services they are paid to do. Immediately after Emergency Services we went to our final spot which was where a statue of the racist mayor of Philly from the 1970s, Mayor Rizzo, was placed, but we will get into that later.

We marched, about 500 of us, which would have been more if not for the rain, which poured at times, for a good half an hour to Emergency Services where speeches were given. Prior to that Reverend Bruce Wight went into the university where the forum was going on and on loud speaker called the comrades to come to the streets and join the march, surprisingly a large amount of the participants came out with us, including members of Code Pink. It was like God was testing our resolve, not just from the rain throughout, but as literally when we arrived at Emergency Services the rain increased and was all out pouring. In the front part of the protest there was children and people on wheelchairs throughout it, both speaking into the loud speaker alongside Cheri for us to move on and what we were fighting for and started various chants, my favorite being, what was written on my sign, which I had tucked away inside my jacket most of the time as I held the PPEHRCs sign in the front, The People United Will Never Be Defeated! Or as they say in Spanish El Pueblo UnidoJamas Sera Vencido!!

The police blocked off the roads but we had our comrades in cars ahead of us, and the police who knew we never asked permission to march, parted ways and let us pass through. I felt proud we were represented as Reverend Bruce Wright, who came up from Florida with us, spoke about how Florida was one of the worse states in treating the poor and how a 93 year old man was arrested for feeding the poor in Fort Lauderdale. Bruce had walked into a workshop prior to that and asked all the comrades present who was for reform, not a single hand was raised, he then asked who was for revolution, where he got a standing ovation of people full of revolutionary enthusiasm, which showed clearly the general sentiments of the people at this particular forum, far more radical then the Left Forums I had been at prior in NY. I thought to myself as we marched how glad I was I decided not to fly back but to stay an extra day to be in the march and return to Florida with my comrades in a van. Among those to speak when we finally reached Emergency Services was an activist from my area I had not met till then, Pedro El Poeta, or Pedro the Poet, who was a rapper activist. Florida was clearly represented in that march.

We then converged on the Rizzo statue, and exposed this old mayor for his racist practices in Philly, this was the man who helped set up the black panther affiliate and activist Mumia, who is still in jail to this day. The city could have money to erect such statues but not to help the poor dying in the streets. As we marched towards Rizzo we say a huge abandoned church, which comes out in the youtube video of the forum which was already released. After a long march I finally made it back to the church in West Kensington where we had been sleeping, to see performances were being set up. Pedro El Poeta was to perform again with his incredible revolutionary energy, as he was on the frontlines of the march, barely rested, and had done a concert alongside Dave his backup singer, the night before. Pedro is originally from Nicaragua, and had migrated to Florida some years prior, he also happens to be a teacher teaching troubled High School students. On the way back in the van I called into a radio program I co host and passed the phone over to Pedro so he could be interviewed. Krown Deon is a rapper activist as well, out of St. Pete, Fl who performed and did the road-trip, I met him prior. Also the next day, this morning, I was on Don's program he co hosts out of Sarasota, Fl. Don 79 years old was also in the march. There was people of all ages and colors present. Don had in fact been to Peru where my father is from, and met Gustavo Gutierrez, the founder of Liberation Theology, Don also knew Dr. King. Right after Don interviewed me he had Bruce Wright himself call in, and we are working here to continue our work and spread the word inspired by the forum in Philly.

While I marched, it was my first major march since Occupy a couple years prior, I thought of all those who died too young, and left behind their legacy for us to fight for. I thought of Anne Frank, of my comrade Marty Droll who I had marched with in Tampa and showed me around Philly in my first trip there, and of my sister Tasha Suarez. I thought how this would inspire my third book and my continued activist work. How this vanguard of people, the downtrodden of society, could come together and make the impossible possible. The theme for the forum was Another World Is Possible, which was a common chant in Occupy. I think not only is another world possible or probable but inevitable, we can be the change, for the very survival of the human species, so that all the sacrifices before us are not in vain and our children and grandchildren can live in a better society, as they deserve better. I fight for the future of my niece and all the unborn children, as we dream for a new society and make this dream a reality. Hope to see you at the World Forum in Montreal next year!"

The forum in Philly was certainly inspirational. And to awaken the masses from their slumber, from their illusions, to confirm what deep down they know, they need inspiration, inspiration brought by activism, by example, by leadership, and organization, a disciplined organized movement where the vanguard is the base.

The particular political philosophy that is needed is Chavism, which is a new ideology and brings left unity not factionalism, hence the United Socialist Party of Venezuela, and SYRIZA, and now Podemos in Spain have continued in that example whether an indignado or an occupier. The following chapter shows what I wrote on my political philosophy for a class.

Chapter 3

ChavismIn the 21st Century

This is my interpretation of Chavism.

My Political Philosophy: Chavism

Intro

- Chavism is a combination of several political and spiritual ideologies adapted to the 21st century. Of course Chavism is based on the political thinking of Hugo Chavez, who was the democratically elected president of Venezuela from 1999-2013 (he died in 2013 in his 50s of cancer). It includes Bolivarianism, Guevarism, Ecosocialism, Democratic Socialism, Trotskyism, and Liberation Theology.

Bolivarianism

- Bolivarianism is based on the political thinking of Simon Bolivar (born in Venezuela 1783-died in Colombia 1830).

- Bolivar led the war for independence from Spain for several countries over the course of 15 years. This included Panama, Colombia, Venezuela, Ecuador, Peru and Bolivia, Bolivia being named after him. This land was 2 times the size of the area conquered by Alexander The Great, only his soldiers liberated, did not conquer. He was called The Liberator. He was also called The Iron Ass for having rode on horseback for an incredible amount of miles, across mountains, and jungles, through snow and tropical climates. Bolivar's ideology was anti imperialism and Pan Americanism.

- Pan Americanism meaning the unity between liberated Latin American nations who were previously under the yoke of Spanish tyranny. Pan Americanism is a lot like Pan Arabism as it was under Nasser. Under the Spanish Empire each country under their control was forbidden from communicating with one another. The Spaniards feared the colonized people would find they had similar problems, and could unite and rebel against Spanish imperialism, which was what ultimately happened. Before civil war split up the Grand Colombia (which included Panama, Colombia , Venezuela and Ecuador as one nation, Bogota being its capital), these nations made revolutionary acts of no longer being divided and conquered, communicating with each other and uniting in armed rebellion against Spain. Events in Europe helped instigate these events, with Napoleon taking over the Spanish Crown for a time, and people in the colonies had to pick sides, the French, Spanish, or independence. The third option finally bore fruit.

- The leader of the movement, a young wealthy Venezuelan, named Simon Bolivar. In the end, Bolivar did not only free his slaves but saw to the abolition of slavery in South America, being proud, he gave all his riches away to the cause refused money offered to him for liberating nations, and died penniless, in exile, in Colombia, in his 40s, giving in to his fatigue after long journeys and battles. Bolivar never had children, but the Venezuelans today, consider themselves the children of Bolivar. It can be said the unity he fought so hard for came finally with the anti American imperialist and Socialist Hugo Chavez about 160 years later when he was elected to power in Venezuela. Chavez had in fact changed the name of Venezuela to the Bolivarian Republic of Venezuela., some say he could be the political reincarnation of Bolivar adapted to the times. Chavez was born poor, was a military man, who came up in the ranks to commander at a young age, he was imprisoned for a short time in the 90s for an attempted coup against a tyrannical government. Upon his release he started a presidential campaign and was elected.

Guevarism

- Guevarism is based on the political thinking of Ernesto Guevara also known by his nom-de-guerre Che Guevara. (Born in Argentina in 1928, died in Bolivia in 1967).

- El Che, was a man born of the upper classes in Argentina who went in the 50s on a motorcycle trip that changed his life forever. Much like when Buddha or Francis of Assisi were exposed to poverty, the conditions of the indigenous people of the continent Che experienced, or who was known as Ernesto then, shocked Che to his core. Che is Argentine slang for pal, and the name caught on when Che a few years after his motorcyle trip with Alberto Granados, which started in Argentina, and ended up in Chile, Peru, Brazil, Colombia and Venezuela, went to Bolivia. On Che's second trip after graduating for medicine in Argentina, he went to Bolivia and witnessed the new government's reforms there, but they did not last long. Then Che went to Guatemala and worked as a doctor for the progressive government of JacoboArbenz. The first of many CIA backed coups in Latin America happened in Guatemala and Che was there to witness it. Initially taking refuge in the Argentine embassy, Che refused to return home, and went on to Mexico, where he eventually met the exiled Castro brothers..Che was part of the expedition returning to Cuba to topple the dictator Batista, who was backed by the US. Che made a decision over the course of the guerrilla fight in the mountains of the Sierra Maestra, he decided rather than to only be a medic, to also take up arms, he was eventually promoted to commander, and led the guerrilla fighters into Havana as Batista fled, in early 1959, he was 30 years old. Che took up many positions in the Cuban government, remarried a Cuban, had children with her, his first wife he had one child with was a Peruvian exile in Mexico.

- In 1965, Che being an internationalist, a revolutionary, influenced by Trotskyism shown to him by Ernest Mendel, much like Chavez was advised by the Trotskyist Alan Woods which helped change his reform of Capitalism stance to a revolutionary stance. Che eventually over ideologically differences and a plan to leave the country to "export the revolution", left Cuba, his family and Fidel, and started his first voyage to the Congo in Africa to defend the rebels who were recently toppled with the CIA backed coup against Lumumba. This mission however failed, Fidel having read after several months of Che'sdisappearence ,Che's farewell letter, Che had to come to Cuba in secret, his next mission, incognito as a Uruguayan businessman, had him go to Bolivia. For 11 months Che and his band of guerrillas of fighters from all over Latin America, fought the government of US backed Barrientos. In the end Che was captured and executed in October 1967. He died at the age of 39 like Martin Luther King, and less than one year before the death of MLK. Chavez often talked of Che, how when he was a soldier he read Che's book "Guerrilla Warfare" and held a secret sympathy for him. Chavez used Che'simage interchangeably with that of Bolivar in his democratic revolution in Venezuela.

Ecosocialism

- Ecosocialism is a type of Socialism with emphasis on the ecology or environment. Chavez's country have regions that were in the Amazon, with Amazonian indigenous people, Chavez was in favor of protecting the people and the jungle areas from destruction, he was against destroying the trees and wanted alternative ways that were progressive to prevent such destruction.

Democratic Socialism

- Democratic Socialism is the belief that Socialism can be acquired through democratic means, such as the recent election of Alexis Tsipras in Greece, a Socialist who intends to end the cuts or austerity on the poor of his nation, or of course the current president of Venezuela, democratically elected Maduro, who has continued the legacy of Chavez in-spite of the saboteurs, Maduro was Chavez's VP. Allende elected in 1971 in Chile and toppled in a US backed coup in 1973, was a Democratic Socialist as well.

- Trotskyism

- Trotskyism is based on the political thinking of Leon Trotsky. Trotsky (born in Ukraine in 1879, died in Mexico in 1940) was a Ukrainian Jew of Russian nationality.

- This is significant since at the time the Jews in Russia were persecuted as what is known as the pogroms, the pogroms were a big inspiration to Hitler and he mentioned them in his book. Trotsky was a Marxist revolutionary Socialist who bravely fought the tyranny of the Czar or King of Russia. He was exiled to Siberia twice, each time escaping, his last escape he was able to go to Europe and meet fellow revolutionaries, including Lenin. By 1917, during WWI of which Russia was a participant, Trotsky had teamed up with Vladimir Lenin as they reunited in Russia when the reformist government of Kerensky took over. Lenin and Trotsky eventually toppled Kerensky, ended Russia's part in WWI, taking over Russia in what is known as the October Revolution, which was actually conducted on Trotsky's birthday. The hammer and sickle on the Soviet flag was Trotsky's idea, Trotsky formed the Red Army, which were originally rag tag soldiers to defend the country from a foreign backed civil war that took place soon after the Bolsheviks took power, Trotsky being a leader of the Bolsheviks. Among nations to send troops and back the White Guards who fought the Red Army, was the US, having sent troops to Ukraine. Inspite of this by the early 1920s Russia's civil war ended. However, Lenin fell ill, and inspite of his political testament siding with Trotsky over Stalin, Stalin brutally took over, went after the Bolsheviks, and reversed the revolution in the name of a degenerated form of Communism, Trotsky being sent to exile in Turkey in 1929, he was finally killed by a Stalinist agent in 1940 in Mexico. Many of Trotsky's followers in his political thinking remain, especially in Latin America, his grandson in Mexico, one of his few family members not killed by Stalin, run's the house where Trotsky went to exile now a museum, and also the spot where Trotsky is buried. Socialism In One Country is an ideology that Stalin brought which conflicted with that of Trotsky, who wanted International Socialism, with the fall of the Soviet Union in the early 90s many Trotskyists saw this as a vindication and a opportunity for Trotskyist, or Trotsky like revolutions to come about such as what was attempted in Spain and Hungary, and what in Bolivia, Venezuela and Greece are being attempted.

Liberation Theology

- Liberation Theology was founded by a Peruvian priest named Gustavo Gutierrez born in 1928, and who is still alive today. It is belief in social justice through progressive Christianity. Many members of the Church, especially in Latin America, have allied with Socialists, even revolutionaries, against tyranny from fascists or others. Lugo of Paraguay is an example of a former head of state who was a priest and part of this movement. They focus on what Jesus said about rich and poor, and how he kicked the moneychangers out of the temple, and called for the end of corruption and the rule of Roman imperialism. They see many of the problems Jesus faced still problems today. Chavez took the best from each philosophy or ideology but did not accept everything in them. For example Marxists believe in dialetical materialism and are therefore atheists. Chavez considered himself Christian, and as such a spiritual person with progressive thought. Bartolome de las Casas it could be argued was of the Liberation school before it existed, he convinced the Spanish crown to end slavery of the indigenous people, but this did not prevent Brazil from continuing it or the importation of black slaves. Regarldess, liberation thinking certainly influenced Chavez.

- Conclusion

- My father being Peruvian and having lived a couple years in Peru and Spain, it gave me insight into different ways of thinking and I have come to accept over the years I am a Chavista, a believer in Chavism. I love my country of birth, the country of my mother's birth, the US. However, imperialism in all its forms I am against. My paternal grandfather like Gutierrez and Che was born in 28' and came from the same generation and culture, which has influenced me. My maternal grandfather was a Russian Jew, and this helped led me to learn about Trotsky, and the people he influences today. This concludes my political philosophy, I hope we have time for questions.

Indeed, you personalize when forming your ideas or ideals based on your experiences and background. Also your philosophy can shown in practice such as the left unity in Latin America in the early 2000s. Not just the democratic route as an alternative to the guerrilla struggle, but militias, such as the Bolivarian militias in Venezuela, which is comprised of many women, can be formed. The contradiction of militia and left common in the US is combated in a piece I wrote and spoke about on the radio called the Left Militia, which is what I will start the next chapter with.

Chapter 4

Left Militia Principles

The Left Militia

Many former members of the Occupy Wall Street such as myself have questioned the tactics used in the movement, which has disintegrated into splinter groups. Not just have we seen the contradictions on leadership and organization, and how both should have been implemented in the movement democratically, but also on the tactics used, their effectiveness, and context. The Bolsheviks had General Assemblies in Russia who openly defied the Czar who had speakers voted democratically to represent their movement, occupy never made this step, and left itself vulnerable to external infiltration. New wave Anarchists and Feminists have prevented the progress on organization and caused division when they exerted their influence in the occupy movement.

The question of non-violence as well, is a continuing one, which sparks debate among many circles, particularly in the left. Often in the US such as the case in "Bundy's Ranch", we hear in the so-called mainstream media, "right-wing nutjobs" interchangeably with the word militia. We also hear the word militia to describe "minority" groups like the Black Panthers, who also have gone into decline, since the 70s.

The idea of the militia is an American phenomenon that dates back to the forming of the country which led to the writing of the Constitution. The right to overthrow, the right to bear arms, are fundamental rights that are guaranteed to American citizens. However, state laws, and different interpretations, have limited these rights over the decades. If we see internationally, how militias have been used, we see many militias, such as in Spain or Latin America, have been used for the left cause. Among these guerrilla or militia leaders the most well known and respected is Che Guevara. We see in Che's "Guerrilla Warfare" a masterpiece on how revolutionaries can accomplish their aims through armed struggle.

If we learned anything from the Ferguson tragedy, we learned protesting peacefully for over 100 days accomplishes nothing but an increase of the Police State, an increase in surveillance, and an increase in no-indictments and impunity of the police. Occupiers non-violently resisting police resulted in 1000s of arrests, including brutal arrests, of which I was arrested twice doing civil disobedience, and resulted in no laws being changed, no demands being met. And consensus through so-called direct or horizontal democracy was not made, autonomous action planned in secret from affinity or working groups had to come about to do certain things, like building improvised barricades to make it harder for police to shut down our camps. But long term solutions were not made.

Nevertheless, it is clear to anyone with eyes to see that non-violence is not effective in America, especially with a corporate media that is subservient to the State, reporters in the end sympathetic to occupy or social justice, human rights in general, in the end were silenced. By 2012 after only a year of the occupy movement, the movement disintegrated. What lessons can we learn from this? If you see my second book "The Unfinished Revolution" I discuss the ideals of the occupy movement and how a new movement can be formed with a change in tactics and with an organizational base or vanguard, led by students and workers, to bring about a revolutionary movement that will leave the reformist centrist position to a more radical militant position.

In the final analysis, not only is it not a contradiction to form a militia and be of the left, it is part of the left tradition. The time for the cancer of pacifism and being passive is over, it is time to make a more aggressive stance. Members of Anonymous if they are serious, should be raising funds to build an army and recruit veterans to train us in these tactics, in focoism, etc, instead of raising money to buy a home and do other bourgeois so-called Anarcho Capitalist things, when revolutionaries are against such private property. Oath Keepers in Ferguson if they are serious, should not follow orders from the police or only concern themselves with protecting property, they should be there to defend the people regardless of color in the face of a Police State. When hesitancy is lifted, and a disciplined militia can be formed, then a party or movement can lead the people of this country to a new American revolution. The founders with all their flaws had the wisdom in their anti British imperialism stance, to assume we would have a revolution every 10 years, the right to overthrow the government, unlike other nations, is literally in our Constitution. Our current corrupt parasitic politicians are afraid of the Constitution, which they swear to defend. Soon their hypocrisy and political cowardice will make them regret, as a peoples tribunal will come, as their popularity decreases, the people can rise up to act upon what they know, to act upon their conscious, and to support a peoples militia, to replace the current system with another, which is more just, humane, and egalitarian for the betterment of society towards a new society. The economic system needed is Socialism, and all left groups need to unite under this banner. A permanent revolution with international backing can happen from this developed nation and spread the world over! Our resolution is revolution, for a better future for our children! A world without classes, division of race or sex!

 In Solidarity,

Al Suarez

12/27/14

Founder of the Revolutionary Liberation Party, USA

Co Host of Voice of Rebellion Radio, UCY (formerly Blogtalkradio)

My party, the RLP, is but of many of the left, we must form all the forces of principle never sacrificing them, whether they abandoned their party or not, those who are loyal to the working class, poor and peasants to build the new society, the counter culture, and the new consciousness. The radical revolution of values of Dr. King, as we marched in the spirit of Dr. King my comrades and me recently in Philly, is still here, next is a paper I wrote for my College on us fulfilling Dr. King's legacy.

Chapter 5

Dream A Reality: Dr. King's Legacy Discussed From Paper and Beyond, Word To Action

"What Would I Personally Do To Help Fulfill Dr. Martin Luther King Jr's Dream, and How Has It Been Fulfilled or Not Fulfilled 50 Years Later?

By Alexander Suarez

ENC 1101

12/9/14

Randy Howard

Last year in August I went to Washington DC for the 50th anniversary of the march on Washington, where King's "I Have A Dream" speech was given. I wrote an article for the Hawkeye Newspaper (HCC's paper) which was selected for the Triad magazine, about this trip, which was a road-trip I took with a couple friends of mine, as we took a few road-trips that year into this year. Rather than quote from the article am going to go briefly into that experience and say what significance it has for the legacy of MLK.

First, in my article I showed an image of Jesse Jackson and Cornel West, Dr West was not invited to speak at the podium, since he is critical of Obama, in particular his drone program, they had met together at a café and I got word of the event at the last moment. I think Dr West is the embodiment of MLK today and I had the pleasure of meeting him and taking a photo with him, many of these photos appeared in the article. At the actual event, there was only about a quarter million that showed up that day, and there was double that 50 years prior. However, the grandchildren of those that were there that day were present and kept up the legacy of King, that of not just racial equality but economic equality, indeed, his last march on Washington he was planning in his last days before his assassination, was one for workers rights. He talked of blacks converging on Washington to demand their paycheck, that is, for reparations for slavery. This side of MLK is not talked about, as statues and busts of MLK are made, a myth of MLK is made, a man who fought exclusively for civil rights, when this is simply not true.

Nevertheless, MLK talked about the three pillars they were fighting, militarism, racism and poverty. Many times the militarism and poverty part are left out. As we see rioting in Ferguson, we remember the words of MLK "Rioting is the language of the unheard." MLK said he refused to condemn his brothers rioting in the ghettos before first condemning the Vietnam War, and the killing of innocent brown babies half a world away. This helped sway US public opinion in the late 60s against the war, the draft, and everything involving the Vietnam intervention, as MLK was a moral force.

Although many people turned against him after that, he admitted in his speech that there were people urging him to stay on civil rights, but MLK could not be silent any longer, his conscious not letting him. He also talked about the military budget, how more and more money that could go to social programs and programs of social uplift, are used instead to bomb other nations. We see that the military budget has increased much more since then. The past decade alone it has doubled to 60% of the national budget, the US spending more on its military than all the nations of the world combined, maintaining its military super power, but at what cost to the economy, and the poor, as the rich do not pay their share, and the middle class continues to shrink in this crisis? MLK was a visionary, a man ahead of his time who saw correlations others did not see, but as a leader, helped opened the eyes of the masses.

In the final analysis, as we see the movie Selma coming out soon about MLK's struggle there, we see many of the same problems we faced in the 60s happening now, indeed the Voting Rights Bill MLK fought so hard for, has already been overturned by the US Supreme Court some months ago. Many of the rights we had in the 60s we have lost, things in many ways have gotten worse, especially when it comes to economic inequality. I think to help fulfill his dream I must help to organize a movement not just to fight for civil rights, but human rights, which is what MLK was fighting for in the end. He said he was fighting for a radical revolution of values. Indeed, not just a physical revolution, but a spiritual revolution of values, of consciousness, of a state of consciousness, is what is needed for the new society our country can bring, which would influence events the world over."

Even the Capitalists if they find profitable making a film will help produce one against their own system such as Selma or letting Michael Moore do his films as he has said something to this effect. However, we must not let racism distract us from the main issue, classicism, and we ultimately strive for a classless society. But without liquidating the entire ruling class we can get our hands on either.

We must also understand the importance of not making the same mistakes made in the French, Russian, Spanish, Cuban and even to an extent, American revolutions (the American one, a young nation, inspiring the French and Russian, as they had happened within a few decades of each other) of killing people for their identity rather than their acts. We must in extreme cases execute, but exile or imprisonment must be considered, and for crimes, not for being members of the aristocracy or bourgeoisie alone. We must be just and humane and Dr. King would attest to this. We can still be militant like Malcolm but without infringing on the human rights of others, or the right to a fair trial whether revolutionary tribunal or not. So the next chapter deals with avoiding these mistakes.

Chapter 6

Avoiding Past Mistakes: Protecting The Rights of the Enemy Class

During the French Revolution as Napoleon who reversed the original intents of the revolution in much of the same style as Stalin, country after country was invaded and new Kings, often of the Bonaparte blood, were put in place against the will of the masses. As propaganda of the "rights of man" of the republic against monarchy, propped up, even Spaniards for example, of a more liberal or freethinking notion sympathetic to the French, resisted the brute force imposed upon Spain, among those were Goya, who despised the Church even though he painted for them. Goya's impression of the French changed, even though he eventually went into exile in France, when he witnessed the brutality, and made paintings exposing the French occupation. From Zaragoza to Madrid, the French and the Egyptian forces Napoleon had assembled, continued to massacre the proud Spanish people, as they used whatever means to resist, such as the subterranean Roman tunnels of Zaragoza where weapons to fight the French were stored, Zaragoza, a city I know well in the heart of Aragon province. The same city where much of the fighting against fascism in the Spanish Civil War happened.

The anti fascist forces I have in the past tended to glorify, but upon more research, found there were many mistakes made, although I overall still support their role in history. If you read a book Orwell recommended, who himself was in the Spanish Civil War as Hemingway was in the Lincoln Brigade Orwell was in the POUM brigade, The Spanish Cockpit, written by a German sociologist (Borkenau) and former Marxist, you see mention of whole villages in the south of Spain (Andalusia) where almost every lawyer was summarily executed, for the mere fact of being a lawyer. The sociologist had no reason to lie about these instances, and Orwell does not dispute them, as he had ample time to do so, not dying till the 1950s. As the author was anti fascist and no Stalinist, in fact like Orwell was persecuted by Stalinists in Spain.

These injustices were used by Franco's forces, a type of fascist force, to rally recruits. Both sides having committed atrocity. The moral high-ground was at times hard to distinguish, and the left should not repeat these mistakes. Che was overzealous you could say in the military tribunals of Havana because of the conditions primarily imposed by US imperialists, however this is not to say it is reflected in the character of Commander Che Guevara and his role in the Cuban Revolution, and the inspiration of Latin American movements in general where he gave the ultimate sacrifice in Bolivia, at the core of South America named after its greatest liberator.

We must, in essence, learn from the mistakes of the past, make the parallels, and prevent these mistakes from recurring. A mistake is an error that needs correction, when the error is not fixed and is intentionally continued it turns to crime, its natural consequence, injustice, which cannot and will not be justified by the vanguard. The enemy class is still human and therefore is entitled to rights and we must not be hypocritical or overzealous in our efforts to punish those who have oppressed us, no matter how hard, but make a disciplined justice that may at times take time. Intimidation of the defense, or press who is sympathetic to the enemy is unacceptable.

We must make both sides heard, therefore the press must also represent the interests of the working class. In Venezuela, for example, most of the press is still a private press and is hostile to democratically elected president Maduro as many stations broadcast from Miami, the southern extreme of the Empire where the hostility of a united Latin America has culminated, including hostility towards Central America as Nicaragua has turned into a base for Honduran exiles and others to re-gather their strengths since the Obama backed coup of democratically elected president Zelaya.

Nevertheless, when democratic means have been exhausted, such as what Zelaya has attempted, militia means must be considered, but with leftist principles and organization. Certain groups of anarchists may disagree, but an organized platform or party, along with a militia to backup the movement, is essential for the survival of the revolutionary group towards the revolutionary society and the survival of the human species in these crucial times.

Chapter 7

Social Democracy VS Democratic Socialism

The Bernie Sanders of the world have been around a long time. The bourgeois reformists who claim to be radical, but are a living contradiction or oxymoron. The want to change the system, but ultimately keep it in fact, work within in, within the Democratic Party, as they stab the working class in the back and go after unions, as the Republicans stab in the front, tend to say what they mean, and are less dangerous as a result. Social Democrats, such as those that assured the victory of the fascists and the defeat of Rosa Luxemburg in Germany, are just as dangerous as Stalinists, and have in the past worked together, in fact at one time Stalin had a pact with Hitler.

An example of a Democratic Socialist, as he expressly calmed himself quite correctly, and is mentioned in my political philosophy paper, is Chavez, where Chavism stems from and takes its principal inspiration who cannot be ignored.

The United Socialist Party of Venezuela was a third party, and Venezuela, being democratic by the late 90s, had, had the masses vote for this Bolivarian leader who would be the early 2000s reveal he became a convinced Socialist, and the masses continued to support him, and international observers like Jimmy

Carter, approved the system that had him elected time and again, a system inspite of sabotaged inspired by US Empire, has continued under Nikolas Maduro as it was under Hugo Chavez. And with leaders like Evo Morales in Bolivia, elected in 2006, and other neighbor brother countries, has continued, representing the indigenous people and downtrodden of society, oppressed since the Spanish invasion.

Chavistas are more than rhetoric, they are about action.Chavism, like the ethnicity of Chavez, is mixed with different principled political thought over the years. My paper on it was in the form of a presentation with the factors of it written on the wall, and although the professor did not necessarily agree with it all or the students were not acquainted, it was well received, for if you are passionate about something people tend to respect your view, if they disagree or are not sure about it. Just as a Zionist does not have to be Jewish to be Zionist a Chavista does not have to be Latin American to be a Chavista. Hate to use this analogy as I am not particularly sympathetic to Zionism but I think it is a good one. The counter culture and the struggle of state channels like Telesur, which have spread to other Latin countries, continues...

Chapter 8

The Counter Media and Counter Culture: The Essence of Revolutionary Change

In order to change the culture there must be a cooperative media, or at least a faction of the media that is on your side. This is not propaganda, but truth, at least your view of the truth and how it is portrayed to the masses. I continue in my studies in College in media, as I have understood from a young age, as I am currently 30, and gone back to College after living abroad, that the role of the media brings the perception to the masses and this power is essential to democracy.

As Dewey the philosopher said, and I am not a liberal like him but have taken from much of what he has said, a democracy will not function well with a people who are not informed, if the corporate media in particular, working with an oppressive government, misinforms the masses, it ceases to be real media and its legitimacy or function has ceased. Dewey Square in Boston is named after this philosopher, native of Vermont, a state I know well. That is the Square where occupy had its camp.

Dewey Commission is also the commission he headed which ultimately exonerated Trotsky from the Stalinist Moscow Trials as they were conducted in Mexico in the 30s in contrast to the steps Stalin was taking to liquidate the Bolshevik old guard. Liberals tend to be centrists or reformists, but Trotsky, a real revolutionary, at the end of the commission's investigation said to Dewey is all liberals were like him he would be a liberal, and Dewey said if all Socialists were like Trotsky he would be one too.

The media must keep the government in check, it is the only profession mentioned in the Constitution and must be respected, and it is continually being violated, even in the US where the illusion of free speech is maintained, the illusion of democracy, what Orwell called a beautiful illusion. Orwell had lived on the streets and wrote a book about it before he became known and done fictions, but based on reality. His perspective was quite unique and he was a revolutionary in his own right.

The alternative media, and social media, is an imperfect media, but certainly tends to be more fair than your average CNN, such as seeing a report from Russia Today or Press TV, or even the American Democracy Now program. Art is also essential to revolution, this includes poetry and music, which was clearly animated in the Philly trip outlined earlier, and will be discussed in the next chapter…

Chapter 9

Building The Revolutionary Art Culture

If you happen to be an artist I suggest you do not skip to this chapter, it is not semi autobiographical as my previous novel was, but it is important to understand context and at first read this from the beginning. I did my first painting when I was three. I have seen young children are protests. I see nothing wrong with this unless the child is coerced or not safe, to start endeavors quite young. Rap and politics, with artists I got to meet in Philly like Immortal Technique, of Peruvian extraction, and Rebel Diaz, of Chilean extraction, epitomize the importance of the youth getting behind the movements, and these artists being utilized as such.

An artist I befriended who came back to Florida with me is known as Pedro El Poeta, AKA Pedro the Poet, of Nicaraguan extraction, he uses bilingual lyrics (English and Spanish) in a similar fashion to the other artists mentioned. An example of an artist from a generation before who was initially radical, named after a Peruvian warrior, a product of Black Panthers, was Tupac Shakur, who was recruited by Dr. Dre who was also an activist against police brutality in the early 90s when he was part of the NWA. Some may say today Dr. Dre is a sellout, but the origins of these artists is indisputable.

The revolutionary energy art brings, as I have witnessed through his performances, helps get the youth and the vanguard together to do marches such as what we did in the streets of Philly that rainy afternoon.Like murals need constructing, such as those made by Diego Rivera, who had hosted Trotsky in his home when he went into Mexican exile, his last exile, as an artist, the art culture needs to define itself and adapt in how to translate to the poor youth in the street, and empower them to action.

Drugs and alcohol may be fun, but when it is time to get serious about reality, the struggle, and confront it rather than escape, when anger, as I have described in other books, can be used constructively instead of riot or random violence, then things can progress.The revolution starts from within our own consciousness, and can be released when we have matured enough and are brave and smart enough to try to implement the common society we seek and go after the common enemy, with principles of love and justice for the new society.

Pre-Conclusion: Thoughts on Comrade Marty

It is not traditional to do a pre conclusion but I think it is needed here. This short novel and yet powerful novel will be probably one of many I will write in my life, who knows when it will end, but I hope my life is one full of enthusiasm. Recently taking a break from study, and losing my job upon return from my trip, I use this time to write. When I had previously taken a trip to Philly a year and a half ago when my dear comrade Marty was still alive, I returned to Tampa only to find out I was kicked out of the club I was president to out of retaliation for my activism.

I remember now I called Marty upset about this, and he was of the most loyal comrades, he would go to court for you, go to battle for you, this type of loyalty today is rare and it was a big loss for me to lose my brother, my comrade of comrades. My second book is dedicated to him and I write this book in the spirit of Marty in the spirit of unity and end it thinking of him and our common cause, our common struggle, may people know the writings and contributions of Marty Droll, and may we learn the truth of how he died.

Conclusion

Che Guevara, Hugo Chavez, Simon Bolivar, Leon Trotsky, and others I have not mentioned but I have read up on and tried to learn from, all were men, and therefore made mistakes, and in my adolescence I tended to glorify some of these men. In-spite of their mistakes, and among the revolutionaries, like Tania who was part of Che's campaign in Bolivia, or Rosa Luxemburg in the German attempt at revolution, I think they exemplified the revolutionary spirit among us all. We strive for a just world, and rather than dream as Quixote did, of that illusion, we strive to make it a reality as Venezuelans, Bolivians, and others are building that new world south of the border and here in the developed society of the empire we can make that change too, which would have repercussions all over the world and internationally would be supported by all the oppressed peoples of the world.

www.ingramcontent.com/pod-product-compliance
Lightning Source LLC
Chambersburg PA
CBHW070944290526
45795CB00003B/1136